Tutankhamun

Gill Harvey

Designed by Karen Tomlins
and Michelle Lawrence

Illustrated by Ian McNee

History consultant: Dr. Anne Millard
Reading consultant: Alison Kelly, Roehampton University

Edited by Jane Chisholm
Cover design by Russell Punter
Cover illustration by Ian Jackson

First published in 2006 by Usborne Publishing Ltd., Usborne House,
83-85 Saffron Hill, London EC1N 8RT, England. www.usborne.com
Copyright © 2006 Usborne Publishing Ltd. The name Usborne and the
devices ♈♈ are Trade Marks of Usborne Publishing Ltd.

ACKNOWLEDGEMENTS
The publishers are grateful to the following organisations for their permission to reproduce material:
© **Alamy**: p2-3 bygonetimes, p33 Mary Evans Picture Library, p40 Popperfoto; © **Corbis**: p1
Royalty-Free, p4-5 © Roger Wood, p31, p37 © Stapleton Collection, p47 Bettmann, p59 © Frank
Trapper, p60-61; © **Getty Images**: p36 © Hulton Archive, p54 © Time & Life Pictures, p58
Rosemary Calvert; © **Griffith Institute, Oxford**: p26, p27, p28, p29, p32, p34-35, p38, p39, p41,
p42, p43, p44, p48, p49, p50, p51, p52, p53, p55, p57; © **The Illustrated London News Picture
Library**: p6; **popperfoto.com**: p30; **TopFoto.co.uk**: p25; **www.araldodeluca.com**: p24
Picture research: Ruth King & Lou Breen

Every effort has been made to trace the copyright holders of material in this book. If any rights
have been omitted, the publishers offer their sincere apologies and will rectify this in any
subsequent editions, following notification.

This is one of a nest of coffins that contained
the mummy of King Tutankhamun.

Contents

Internet links

You can find out more about Tutankhamun by going to the
Usborne Quicklinks Website at
www.usborne-quicklinks.com
and typing in the keyword "Tutankhamun".

At the Usborne Quicklinks Website you will find direct
links to a selection of recommended websites.
Here are a few of the things you can do:

• Unwrap an Egyptian mummy.
• Discover what the young king actually looked like.
• See photographs of Tutankhamun's treasures.

The recommended websites are regularly reviewed and updated
but, please note, Usborne Publishing is not responsible for the
content of any website other than its own.

This aerial view shows the Valley of the Kings outside
Luxor, Egypt. Many Egyptian kings were buried here
in rock-cut tombs, which were then deliberately
hidden to protect their treasures from robbers.

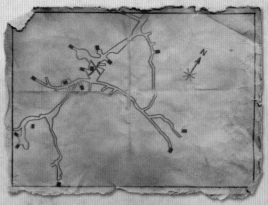

This archaeologist's sketch shows the locations of royal tombs in the Valley of the Kings. The entrance to Tutankhamun's tomb is marked with a cross.

Chapter 1

Wonderful things

Howard Carter took a deep breath and mopped his forehead, squinting up at the limestone cliffs that towered above the Valley of the Kings. It was February 1922 and this was the moment he'd been waiting for. He had spent five long years in this dry desert, searching for the tomb of the ancient Egyptian king, Tutankhamun. Now it looked as if he'd finally found it...

But he couldn't be sure. He had found a mysterious doorway that seemed to be the entrance to a tomb. Behind it, there was just a corridor full of rubble, and Carter still didn't know what lay beyond it.

A workman ran up to him, panting. "We've finished clearing the rubble," he said. "And we've found another doorway!"

Howard Carter (in the white shirt) stands with Lady Evelyn Herbert, Lord Carnarvon and Arthur Callender outside the entrance to Tutankhamun's tomb. This photograph was taken in November 1922, shortly after the tomb was first opened.

Carter turned to his patron, Lord Carnarvon. "This is the moment of truth," he said, his voice trembling.

Carter led the way along the gloomy corridor, followed by Lord Carnarvon and his daughter Lady Evelyn. While they looked on anxiously, he made a small hole in the doorway. Then he lit a candle and put it through the hole. The flame flickered for a second, but then burned brightly. Gripping the candle tightly to calm his nerves, Carter put his eye to the hole. He seemed to stand there forever, just staring and staring.

Lord Carnarvon grew restless. "Well," he snapped, "can you see anything?"

Carter turned, his face stunned with shock.

"Wonderful things!" he finally managed to whisper.

"Wonderful things!"

7

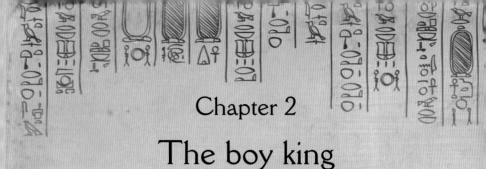

Chapter 2

The boy king

Over three thousand years earlier, the people of Egypt woke up one morning to find that Tutankhaten, a nine-year-old prince, had become king – or pharaoh.

The government officials were delighted. "He's only a boy," they said to each other. "We can boss him around easily!" Excitedly, they set to work, listing all the things they wanted to change. Thanks to the previous king, Akhenaten, it was a pretty long list.

Akhenaten had introduced some very unpopular ideas in his seventeen-year reign. For one thing, he had made drastic changes to the Egyptian religion. Instead of worshipping whichever god took their fancy, the Egyptians were ordered to worship only one: Aten, the shining sphere of the Sun.

Not everyone liked the idea, and the priests
of Amun – who had been the chief god
until then – were appalled.

9

But Akhenaten didn't care – he just went on making changes. He decided to build an entirely new town filled with beautiful palaces and temples, all dedicated to the god Aten. He named his town Akhetaten and sited it on a dusty desert plain (where the village of Amarna is today), far away from the temples of Amun at Thebes.

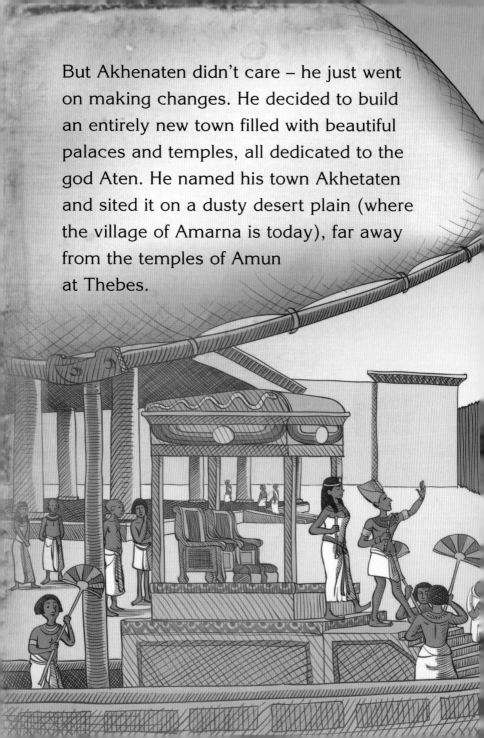

Akhenaten had an effect on Egyptian art styles too. Artists exaggerated the king's features, and painted and sculpted him with a long, thin face, bulbous head and bulging belly. Soon it became fashionable for people to have themselves painted in the same strange style.

By the time Akhenaten died, the country was in a mess. The king had been far too busy with all his new ideas to run it properly, and everyone was longing for a return to the old ways.

Prince Tutankhaten, Akhenaten's son by his second wife, Queen Kiya, was the only available heir. But he was much too young to rule alone, so he was going to need government ministers to help him.

Tutankhaten probably didn't have much say over what happened next. His ministers seem to have wasted no time in moving the court back to Thebes.

"If we're going to move back to Thebes, I suppose I'd better change my name too?" sighed the young king.

"Good idea," said his advisers. "How about Tutankh*amun*? That will make you popular with the priests of Amun!"

It made perfect sense, so the name stuck.

Chapter 3

A tomb in the rocks

Very quickly, things returned to normal. The city of Akhenaten was swiftly abandoned, to be covered by drifting sands. Tutankhamun married his half-sister, Ankhesenamun, and settled down to do what so many Egyptian kings had done before him: he started some grand building projects. Although he was still a child, the most important of these was his tomb.

Not surprisingly, he wanted to be buried with his ancestors, in a desert valley opposite Thebes, on the west bank of the river Nile – the place we call the Valley of the Kings. For hundreds of years, the kings of Egypt had been buried there. Each one had his own tomb, cut deep into the rock and crammed with all the things he would

need in the next life – furniture, food and
lots of gold and jewels. The kings' bodies
were embalmed to make them last forever,
and they were given a lavish funeral.

But long before the workmen had
finished building his tomb, the young king
was dead – at the age of only nineteen.

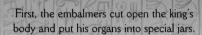

First, the embalmers cut open the king's body and put his organs into special jars.

Next, they covered it all over with a salt, called natron, to dry it out.

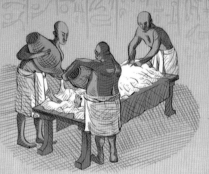

Tutankhamun's tomb wasn't ready – so the courtiers had to think fast. They found another tomb – one that had been built for an official. It wasn't nearly as big as the one the king had been building for himself, and none of the rooms had been painted yet. But it would have to do.

While the country went into mourning, the embalmers set to work on the king's body. First they cut him open and took out

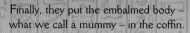

Then they wound layers of bandages around the body very tightly.

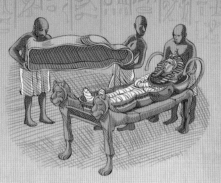

Finally, they put the embalmed body – what we call a mummy – in the coffin.

his internal organs, putting them into special containers called canopic jars. Then they drained his brain out through his nostrils, dried out his whole body with a special salt called natron and treated it with oils and ointments.

When the body was dry enough, they wrapped it tightly in linen bandages. After 70 days, the king was ready for his final journey – to the Next World.

So far, so good. Artists set to work painting the burial chamber as fast as they could – but there was only time to complete three of the walls very sketchily.

Then Tutankhamun was placed inside a nest of beautiful coffins and given a proper state funeral. A procession of mourners carried him up to the desert valley and placed him inside the tomb, along with food, furniture, clothes and treasures – everything he would need in the Next World.

But the tomb was far too small to fit it all in, so everything was all piled up untidily on top of each other.

Tutankhamun didn't have any sons, so there was probably a power struggle over who should rule after him. An old man named Ay became the next pharaoh. He had been one of Tutankhamun's chief advisers, and he may have been the queen's grandfather too.

Chapter 4

Missing

Years passed, and Tutankhamun faded from memory. New generations of kings took his place, and built bigger, better tombs in the valley. One of them, Ramesses VI, had his tomb built just above Tutankhamun's, and his builders let stone chippings fall right over the entrance to the boy king's tomb. That is probably what kept it safe.

Right from the earliest times, the kings of Egypt had

had a problem with tomb robbers. Even when they had been buried in huge pyramids, thieves found their way in to steal the treasure. To begin with, the Valley of the Kings was very well guarded. But later, when the police had become less efficient, thieves moved in.

Before long, the heavy stone coffins and beautiful painted walls were the only things left. All the treasure had gone.

Well, almost...

After most of the tombs had been
ransacked, nobody thought much about
them for ages – for over 3,000 years, in
fact. Then, about 200 years ago, explorers
from Europe began to get interested in
Egypt again. They started poking around
and digging for objects in the desert sand.

Before long, everyone wanted a piece of
ancient Egypt. They wanted to know more
about this amazing culture. Who had ruled
it? Why were there so many mummies and
tombs? Who were all the strange gods that
they worshipped? And what did that
extraordinary picture writing mean?

Piece by piece, scholars put together the answers, and the story of ancient Egypt came to life. There were tales of mighty battles, countless gods and goddesses, and great adventures.

People who studied Ancient Egypt became known as Egyptologists. They found out who all the Egyptian kings had been, and when they had ruled. After years of searching, they had found a tomb for almost all the important kings.

But there was one king who didn't seem to have a tomb anywhere. That king was Tutankhamun.

Experts searched the Valley of the Kings from top to bottom – but by the early 20th century most of them had given up and moved on to other projects. Only one man was still convinced the tomb was there, hidden among the rocks – and that was Howard Carter.

Carter was a very careful thinker. He wasn't just acting on a hunch. Explorers had already found a cup, a box and some jars with the king's name on them.

"The tomb must be here – somewhere!" he reasoned.

This golden mask was found in the Valley of the Kings in 1907, in a pit containing items with Tutankhamun's name on them.

A photograph of Howard Carter taken in 1922

But digging for tombs cost money, so he needed help. In 1917, back home in England, he decided to approach his old friend and colleague Lord Carnarvon. Carnarvon was rich, and he liked dabbling in Egyptology too. When Carter told him about the tomb, he was very enthusiastic.

"Tutankhamun? Sounds wonderful!" he cried. "Don't worry about the cost. Just go ahead and dig."

Chapter 5

One last chance

Carter was delighted. He hurried out to Egypt to start digging in the Valley of the Kings. But it wasn't as easy as he'd hoped. A whole year passed, and there was no sign of the tomb. A second year went by… no tomb. Three more years of digging, and still no tomb.

By 1922, Carnarvon was growing impatient. He called Carter back to England.

Local workers like these helped remove thousands of tons of rock from the Valley during Carter's search for the tomb of Tukankhamun.

Carter took this photograph of the excavations
in the Valley of the Kings in January 1920.

"You'll have to stop," he said bluntly.
"You've been at it for five years and what
have you found? Nothing!"

But Carter was desperate not to give up.
"There's just one more place I must look,"
he said. "Please give me one more year."

"All right then," Lord Carnarvon sighed.
But it's your last chance this time."

"Thank you!" cried Carter. And he raced
back to Egypt as fast as he could.

This photograph shows the entrance to Ramesses VI's tomb. The arrow points to Tutankhamun's tomb, which is hidden under the rocks.

On his first day of work, Carter gathered his workmen in the middle of the Valley. He pointed to some old, broken-down huts.

"Clear those huts away," he said. "I think they may be hiding something..."

So the workmen began to dig. Then, on the third day, a man's shovel hit something hard. Could it be a step?

"Mr. Carter!" he called out. "I think I've found something!"

Carter could feel his hands trembling with excitement.

"Keep digging!" he cried. "Just keep digging!"

The men uncovered another step, and another, until they could see a complete stairway leading to a sealed door at the bottom. Carter stepped down, holding his breath, and examined the seals. He could hardly believe what he saw. There was a name – and the name was Tutankhamun.

Carter rushed to send a telegram to Lord Carnarvon. "At last have made wonderful discovery in Valley. Congratulations!"

These photographs show how the entrance to the tomb looked when it was first discovered in 1922.

Howard Carter (left) meets Lord Carnarvon (right) and Lady Evelyn
Herbert as they arrive at Luxor station on November 23, 1922.

Travel took a long time in those days –
Lord Carnarvon couldn't just hop on a
plane. So Carter had to wait almost three
weeks for him to make his way from
England, accompanied by his daughter,
Lady Evelyn. It was an agonizing wait.

But at last they arrived, and Carter took
them up to the Valley of the Kings.

"Let's get started!" he urged, trying not
to sound nervous. Then he gestured at the
waiting workmen to begin.

Lord Carnarvon and Lady Evelyn were as

excited as Carter was. All three held their breath as the men smashed through the door. Then they peered inside.

"Oh! It's just a corridor," exclaimed Lord Carnarvon, deeply disappointed. "And it's full of rubble."

But Carter had a gleam in his eye. "Don't worry; that's a good sign," he said. "It means the tomb might have been left untouched for centuries."

Then he turned to the workmen. "Keep on digging!" he ordered.

Carter was right. There, at the end of the corridor, was the second door...

Carter, Carnarvon and Lady Evelyn outside the entrance to Tutankhamun's tomb

There was a little hole in the door, which Carter peeked through. Then he enlarged it so that he and Lord Carnarvon could clamber inside. As they stared around them, their mouths dropped open.

The room was piled high with some of the most amazing and beautiful objects they had ever seen.

This is the extraordinary sight that greeted Carter and Carnarvon when they crawled through the second door of Tutankhamun's tomb.

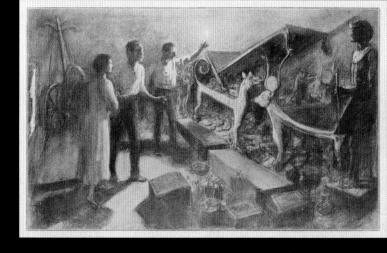

Howard Carter, Lord Carnarvon and Lady Evelyn stare
in amazement at the riches inside Tutankhamun's tomb.

There were almost unbelievable
treasures: beds and couches, an
astonishing throne, painted caskets,
elegant vases, chariots, jewels and
furniture, all covered with gold...

It was too much to take in all at once.
And what seemed even more incredible
was that all these riches had belonged to
just one young boy. It was the discovery of
the century.

The room contained parts of royal chariots and seats covered in gold.

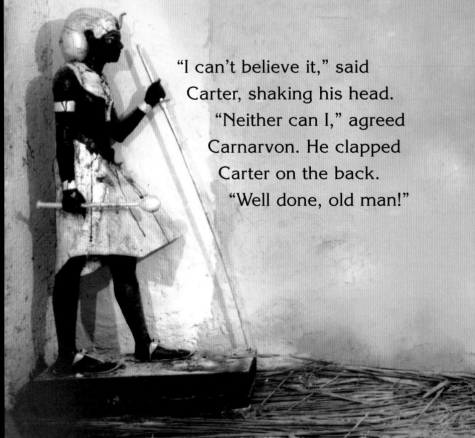

"I can't believe it," said Carter, shaking his head. "Neither can I," agreed Carnarvon. He clapped Carter on the back. "Well done, old man!"

Then, as they gazed around at all the beautiful things, they noticed something else. There were two black and gold statues standing opposite each other, like two eerie watchmen. And on the wall between them, there was a rough square shape in the plaster.

"Could be a doorway," murmured Carter.

"A doorway!" echoed Carnarvon.

He mopped his forehead in disbelief. "You don't think…? You mean there might be more?"

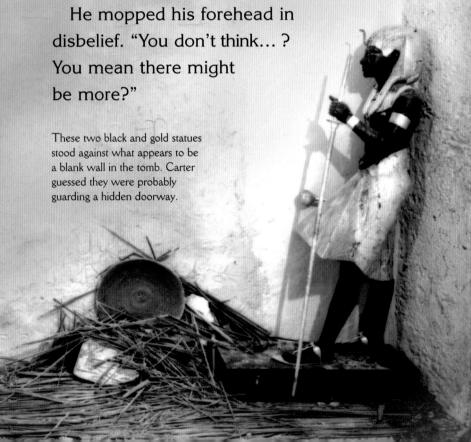

These two black and gold statues stood against what appears to be a blank wall in the tomb. Carter guessed they were probably guarding a hidden doorway.

Carter nodded, but he was beginning to come to his senses. They had a job to do – the biggest job he had ever taken on in his entire career.

"Yes," he said. "But we have to go one step at a time. We can't go through that door until we've recorded everything in here and taken care of it properly."

Lord Carnarvon sighed. Carter was horribly sensible sometimes. "Hmm," he agreed. "I suppose you're right."

Two of Carter's colleagues – Arthur Mace and Alfred Lucas – examine part of a royal chariot after it's been removed from Tutankhamun's tomb.

A worker carries a wooden carving of the head of Tutankhamun, followed by an Egyptian soldier. Soldiers kept a constant guard over the priceless treasures.

And so the work began. Before touching anything, Carter hired a photographer, named Harry Burton, to take pictures of the room just as they'd found it.

Then, one by one, the objects were carried outside. It was a tricky operation. Carter was terrified the fragile treasures would crumble to dust – after all, they hadn't seen daylight for thousands of years. But a team of experts was on hand in a nearby tomb to begin the task of preservation, and very little was lost.

After seven long, tiring weeks, the first room was empty at last.

The first room and its treasures had been one of the most astonishing discoveries of all time. Just one of the golden beds or chariots would have been exciting enough – but a whole roomful was mind-boggling. Carter hardly dared to imagine what he would find beyond the next door.

The truth surpassed his wildest dreams.

Howard Carter (on the right) and Lord Carnarvon begin the careful job of opening Tutankhamun's burial chamber.

28

This is the astonishing sight that greeted
Howard Carter as he peered into the royal burial
chamber – a huge wooden shrine covered in gold.

"It's... it's... a wall of gold!" he stuttered.

That was certainly what it looked like.
When Carter and Carnarvon squeezed into
the room, they could see that the gold wall
was part of a vast golden shrine.

Carter thought of all the other, empty
tombs that lay within the valley, and shook
his head sadly. If even this half-forgotten
boy king had been buried with so many
riches, what had the greatest kings' tombs
been like before they were robbed?

The shrine was actually made of wood covered in gold. Carter squeezed himself around it carefully, gazing at the intricate carvings. Then he spotted something else. There was another doorway, leading off the room – and it wasn't even plastered up. He stepped towards it, his heart pounding...

The first thing he saw was something that looked like a spooky black dog with tall pointed ears, staring straight at him.

This is the statue of the jackal-headed god Anubis, that Carter found in the room next to the burial chamber.

This large shrine, discovered close to Tutankhamun's burial chamber, contained the embalmed internal organs of the young king.

"Anubis!" exclaimed Carter.

It was a striking statue of the god of the dead, mounted on a shrine, with a linen shawl around his shoulders. And behind the statue was yet another shrine, completely covered in gold and surrounded by golden statues of goddesses. Carter could scarcely believe his eyes.

Model boats like this one were placed in the tomb, to help carry Tutankhamun to the Next World.

The room was stuffed full of model boats, caskets, statues and much, much more. Carter was beginning to feel almost panicky. Finding buried treasure was all very well, but he knew that sorting it out and preserving it wasn't going to be easy.

"This job is going to take years!" he muttered to himself.

But there was no doubt that he was the best man for the job. Most people simply didn't have the patience.

And so the work continued.

Howard Carter (in the white shirt) supervises the delicate removal of Tutankhamun's burial treasures from his tomb. Every object was carefully wrapped to protect it as it was moved. Then they were all taken to a laboratory to be cleaned and studied.

Chapter 6

A mosquito bite

Not long after the first room had been cleared, Lord Carnarvon was bitten by a mosquito, right in the middle of his cheek. It happened often enough in Egypt's hot climate, so he tried to ignore the itchy little bump. But then, a few days later, he cut it by accident while he was shaving. Before he knew it, the bite had become badly infected.

Lord Carnarvon was not a

Lord Carnarvon rests at Howard Carter's house outside Luxor. Shortly after this picture was taken, he became seriously ill.

strong man. He tended to fall sick easily, and he quickly came down with a fever.

"You must rest, Father," Lady Evelyn told him. "Please don't push yourself."

"Rest!" he exclaimed. "How can I possibly rest when there's the rest of the tomb to explore?"

"The tomb can wait," insisted Lady Evelyn. So, feeling very grumpy, Lord Carnarvon went to bed. But he was determined not to miss out on the fun. In a couple of days, he was back on his feet and up in the Valley of the Kings again.

But it was too much. It made him feel terrible – much worse than he'd felt before.

"This isn't funny, Father," said Lady Evelyn, once he'd staggered home. "You're really not well. We're going back to Cairo. You need a hospital and doctors."

Lord Carnarvon was forced to agree but, sadly, it was already too late. He had developed pneumonia.

After Lord Carnarvon's death in April 1923,
newspapers like this began to ask if he had fallen
victim to the 'pharaoh's curse'.

Within three weeks, he was dead.

Howard Carter was devastated. Lord
Carnarvon had been his friend, who had
stuck by him for all those years he'd spent
hunting for the tomb. And, what was worse,
the newspapers began to go wild. They
were already impatient to know what else
was in the tomb. Now they had something
really sensational to write about!

"The tomb is cursed!" they cried.

Inside Tutankhamun's shrine, the excavators discovered this stone sarcophagus decorated with images of Egyptian gods and goddesses. The winged arms are meant to be protecting the king's body inside.

Eventually, he was left with nothing but a sarcophagus – a huge stone coffin – just as the ancient Egyptians had left it.

Carter and his team gazed at the granite sarcophagus. "We're going to meet the king at last," he breathed in awe.

Here, the lid of Tutankhamun's coffin is carefully raised, giving the first tantalizing glimpse of what lies beneath.

"But how?" asked one of the men. "That lid must weigh a ton."

In fact, it weighed a ton and a quarter. After scratching his head for a long time, Carter decided what to do. They levered up the edges, then slipped ropes underneath and attached them to pulleys. A group of important officials gathered in the tomb to catch their first glimpse of the king.

They watched eagerly as the pulleys creaked into action. The lid rose slowly into the air. At first, the inside of the sarcophagus looked black – just chips of granite scattered over a rotting linen cloth. But then Carter stepped forward and carefully rolled back the cloth.

Everyone gasped.

An enormous coffin lay before them, with a beautiful carved face covered in shimmering, glittering gold.

When the lid of the king's sarcophagus was finally heaved open, it revealed this spectacular gold coffin inside.

The coffin was huge – much too big for a small mummy.

"There must be other coffins inside it!" exclaimed Carter excitedly.

And that's exactly what they found. There were three coffins altogether, each one fitting snugly inside the next. The second coffin was similar to the first. It was made of wood covered in gold, but it was even more beautiful – with red, blue and turquoise glass inlaid in wonderful patterns.

Carter brushes dust delicately from the surface of Tutankhamun's second coffin. The process took a lot of care and patience.

Using a pulley system, Carter lifted and separated the coffins. But, for some reason, the third one seemed much heavier than the others. It was only after removing the second one that Carter realized why.

Here, a complex system of ropes and pulleys is used to lift the middle coffin from the outer one.

"It's made of solid gold!" he gasped. "That's why it's so heavy!"

When Carter first made the news public, some people didn't believe him.

"Solid gold? Impossible!" they scoffed.

But Carter was absolutely right. And the best was still to come.

The third coffin was covered in horrible sticky stuff. It took Carter ages to clean it all off, although he was dying to see what was inside it.

At last, he'd finished. "Surely there won't be another coffin!" he thought to himself. "This time, we'll find the king himself."

Slowly, carefully, he and his men lifted the lid of the amazing gold coffin... and, sure enough, there was the mummy of Tutankhamun, lying peacefully with his arms crossed over his chest.

Howard Carter studies the mummy of King Tutankhamun after its removal from the tomb.

His hands were covered in gold, and hundreds of jewels and lucky charms were scattered over his body. Over the king's head there was a gold mask, inlaid with precious stones.

Carter was struck dumb. It was the most stunning treasure of all, far more beautiful than anything he had ever seen before.

And the rest of the world had never seen anything like it either.

This photograph shows the mummy of Tutankhamun as Howard Carter first saw it – covered in jewels and wearing a mask of solid gold.

55

Chapter 8

The mummy's secrets

Now that all the treasure had been found, it was time to take a close look at the mummy itself. To help him, Carter hired experts who knew all about bodies. They cut away the linen bandages and examined the body thoroughly.

"He was definitely young when he died," said one expert. "Eighteen, twenty, perhaps. No more."

"But how did he die?" asked Carter. "Why did he die so young?"

The expert shook his head. "I really can't say. The mummy's in pretty poor shape.

We'll probably never know for sure."

When the body was X-rayed, something interesting showed up: there were two tiny pieces of broken bone inside the skull. Did this suggest the young king had been murdered – perhaps by a violent blow to the head?

It was a tantalizing theory. But, later, archaeologists were able to show that these bits had just been broken during the embalming process.

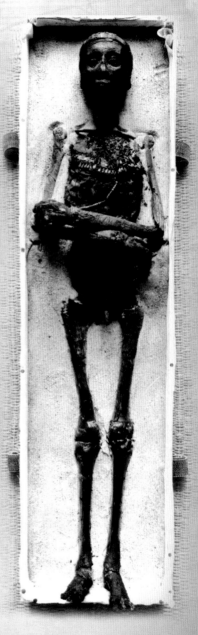

This is how Tutankhamun's body looked once the bandages had been taken off. The hot, dry desert air of the Valley of the Kings had preserved it, even after 3,000 years.

Tutankhamun's burial mask is one of the most famous
archaeological discoveries ever made.

Carter's great task was finally coming to
an end. It had taken him ten long years to
sort out the tomb. He had done a fantastic

job – but, all the same, he felt oddly tired and disappointed.

In 1932, he sailed home to England, worn out. Finding the tomb had made him rich and famous, but it had all been far too much work for one man. He died only seven years later, in 1939.

But the good news was that Egypt now had a magnificent collection of treasures to show the world. Most of it was sent up to Cairo by boat, where it was put on display in the museum. You can still see it there today.

This is a close-up photograph of the front of Tutankhamun's crown, showing the heads of a vulture and a snake. These were symbols of the goddesses who protected the king.

Tutankhamun's mummy was left in the tomb, where it belonged. Today, if you visit the Valley of the Kings, opposite the town of Luxor, on the River Nile, it's possible to peer into the burial chamber, and see the outer coffin where the king still lies.

This is the burial chamber in the tomb of Tutankhamun as you can see it today. The king's outer coffin lies exactly where Howard Carter first discovered it.

This is how the contents of the tomb were arranged when Howard Carter first excavated it. All the treasures are now in the Egyptian Museum in Cairo.

This small room off the antechamber was crammed full of royal furniture, food and wine, and jars of precious ointments and oils.

The antechamber was piled high with gold-covered furniture, chests and dismantled chariots. Two statues guarded the door leading to the burial chamber.

The burial chamber was completely filled by a nest of four huge gold-covered wooden shrines, decorated all over with pictures and hieroglyphs. Right in the middle was the stone coffin containing Tutankhamun's body.

A magnificent statue of Anubis, the god of the dead, guarded the entrance to the treasury. This room contained jewel chests, model boats and a golden shrine containing the king's internal organs.

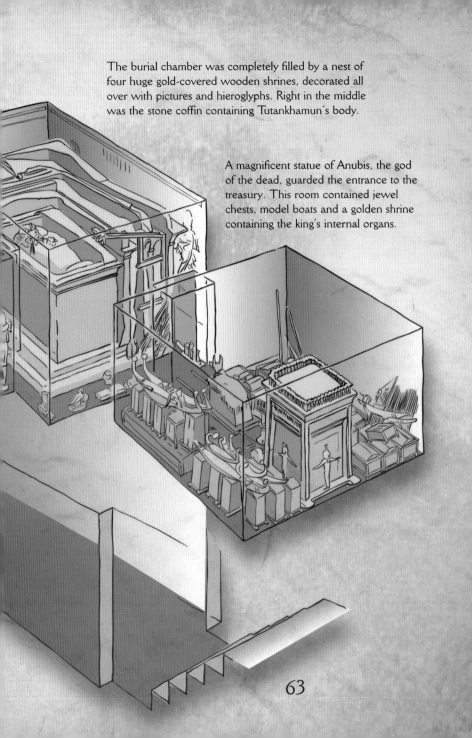

Tutankhamun timeline

c.1347BC* – Tutankhamun becomes King of Egypt.

c.1337BC – Tutankhamun dies and is buried in the Valley of the Kings.

c.1319BC – Tutankhamun's tomb is first robbed, but the robbers only get as far as the antechamber and the small room next to it.

c.1151BC – Workmen digging a tomb for Ramesses VI accidentally bury the entrance to Tutankhamun's tomb with rubble.

c.1000BC – The royal tombs in the Valley of the Kings are dismantled and the contents reburied.

1922 – Howard Carter begins excavations at the site of Tutankhamun's tomb.

1923 – The burial chamber is opened. Lord Carnarvon dies.

1924 – Tutankhamun's stone sarcophagus is opened.

1925 – The inner coffin is opened, revealing the king's mummy.

1932 – Conservation work on the treasures from the tomb is completed, and they are sent to the Cairo Museum.

1939 – Howard Carter dies.

2005 – Further X-rays and examinations reveal new discoveries about the king's death. It appears he died from natural causes – not murder as had once been suggested.

*Dates beginning with c. are approximate dates only.
c. stands for *circa*, Latin for "about". BC means "Before Christ". BC dates are counted backwards from the year 0.